A Guide to AMERICAN STATES

Colorado

THE CENTENNIAL STATE

MEDIA ENHANCED BOOKS

AV²
BY WEIGL

ADDED VALUE • AUDIO VISUAL

www.av2books.com

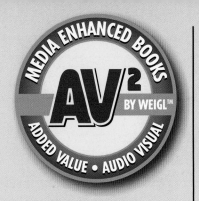

AV² provides enriched content that supplements and complements this book. Weigl's AV² books strive to create inspired learning and engage young minds in a total learning experience.

Your AV² Media Enhanced books come alive with...

Go to **www.av2books.com,** and enter this book's unique code.

BOOK CODE

C 4 9 6 6 8 2

AV² by Weigl brings you media enhanced books that support active learning.

Audio
Listen to sections of the book read aloud.

Video
Watch informative video clips.

Embedded Weblinks
Gain additional information for research.

Try This!
Complete activities and hands-on experiments.

Key Words
Study vocabulary, and complete a matching word activity.

Quizzes
Test your knowledge.

Slide Show
View images and captions, and prepare a presentation.

... and much, much more!

Published by AV² by Weigl
350 5th Avenue, 59th Floor
New York, NY 10118
Website: www.av2books.com   www.weigl.com

Library of Congress Cataloging-in-Publication Data

McLuskey, Krista, 1974-
 Colorado / Krista McLuskey.
   p. cm. -- (A guide to American states)
 Includes index.
 ISBN 978-1-61690-778-5 (hardcover : alk. paper) -- ISBN 978-1-61690-453-1 (online)
 1. Colorado--Juvenile literature. I. Title.
 F776.3.M383 2011
 978.8--dc22
                              2011018317

Printed in the United States of America in North Mankato, Minnesota

052011
WEP180511

Project Coordinator Jordan McGill
Art Director Terry Paulhus

Contents

AV² Book Code 2

Introduction 4

Where Is Colorado? 6

Mapping Colorado 8

The Land 10

Climate 12

Natural Resources 14

Plants 16

Animals 18

Tourism 20

Industry 22

Goods and Services 24

American Indians 26

Explorers 28

Early Settlers 30

Notable People 32

Population 34

Politics and Government 36

Cultural Groups 38

Arts and Entertainment 40

Sports 42

National Averages Comparison 44

How to Improve My Community 45

Exercise Your Mind! 46

Words to Know / Index 47

Log on to www.av2books.com 48

The roof of Denver International Airport was designed to look like snowy mountain peaks.

Introduction

"Go West, young man," wrote a famous newspaper reporter in the mid-1800s, when gold and silver were attracting prospectors to Colorado. Today, many individuals still follow that advice. Whether people go to Colorado for business or pleasure, this western state remains a land of promise, as it was during the days of the gold rush.

Tourists visit Colorado to relax and enjoy the beauty of nature, often in the state's Rocky Mountain recreation areas. Colorado has the highest average **elevation** in the nation. The entire state is 3,300 feet or more above sea level, and its many ski slopes attract skiers by the millions. Skiing, rock climbing, and camping are just a few of the activities that both visitors and residents enjoy.

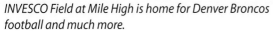

INVESCO Field at Mile High is home for Denver Broncos football and much more.

Breckenridge is one of many well-known ski resorts in the state.

Meeting the visitors' needs has helped shape the state's economy. The large numbers of tourists and business people who go to Colorado create a high demand for hotels and restaurants. Accommodating the travelers has made Denver International Airport among the busiest in the world.

Tourism employs many Coloradans, as do other service industries, such as finance, health care, education, sports, and entertainment. Colorado also supports a wide variety of product-based industries, including mining and agriculture. In addition, the U.S. Army and Air Force have large presences in the area, and many military personnel train and work in the state.

Where Is Colorado?

Colorado is located in the west-central part of the United States. The state's central location in the nation is one reason a number of large companies have based their headquarters within Colorado's borders.

On a map, it is apparent that Colorado is almost a perfect rectangle. But the state's rugged landscape is not made up of straight lines. Two-thirds of Colorado is dominated by jagged mountains and plateaus. The rest of this mountainous state contains rolling foothills and sweeping plains. Although by size Colorado is the 8th largest state, Colorado's population ranks only 22nd in the nation. With so many mountains and protected parklands, much of the land remains unoccupied.

The landscape of Rocky Mountains National Park was formed by glaciers. When the masses of moving ice melted, they dropped the rocks they had been carrying. The park is considered a treasure-trove for rock study.

The Continental Divide runs through the Rocky Mountains in Colorado. East of the divide, rivers flow toward the Atlantic Ocean and Gulf of Mexico. West of the divide, rivers flow toward the Pacific Ocean and Gulf of California.

Thousands of years ago, the grassy plains of Colorado were occupied by grazing bison, often called buffalo. The animals drew the first human inhabitants to the area. The bison were hunted for their meat and hides.

The first signs of human existence in the state date back more than 10,000 years. Prehistoric spearheads have been discovered near piles of bison bones. This finding suggests that the early Coloradans were migratory hunters. They seem to have followed their source of food from place to place, without making permanent homes.

I DIDN'T KNOW THAT!

Colorado is divided into 63 counties.

The land area of Colorado is 103,718 square miles.

The highest peak in the state is Mount Elbert. The mountain stands 14,433 feet above sea level.

Colorado became a state in 1876. The 38th state to enter the Union, it was known as the Centennial State because the Declaration of Independence had been signed 100 years prior.

More than 3 million acres of Colorado land are used for farming.

Mapping Colorado

Located in the west-central region of the United States, Colorado is bordered by Nebraska and Wyoming to the north, Nebraska and Kansas to the east, Oklahoma and New Mexico to the south, and Utah to the west. Colorado's major rivers are the Rio Grande, the Platte, the Arkansas, and the Colorado. The Colorado River flows southwest. After leaving Colorado, it passes through the Grand Canyon, in Arizona, and flows to Mexico, emptying into the Gulf of California.

Sites and Symbols

STATE SEAL
Colorado

STATE BIRD
Lark Bunting

STATE FLOWER
White and Lavender Columbine

STATE FLAG
Colorado

STATE ANIMAL
Rocky Mountain Bighorn Sheep

STATE TREE
Colorado Blue Spruce

Nickname The Centennial State

Motto *Nil Sine Numine*
(Nothing Without Providence)

Song "Where the Columbines Grow," words and music by A. J. Fynn; "Rocky Mountain High," words by John Denver and music by Mike Taylor

Entered the Union August 1, 1876, as the 38th state

Capital Denver

Population (2010 Census) 5,029,196 Ranked 22nd state

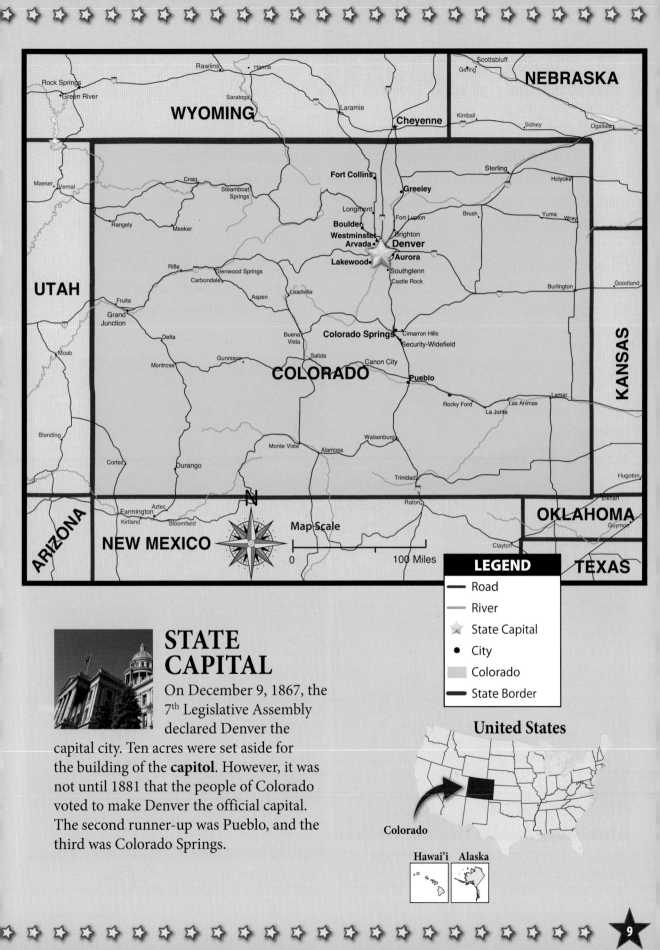

STATE CAPITAL

On December 9, 1867, the 7th Legislative Assembly declared Denver the capital city. Ten acres were set aside for the building of the **capitol**. However, it was not until 1881 that the people of Colorado voted to make Denver the official capital. The second runner-up was Pueblo, and the third was Colorado Springs.

LEGEND

— Road
— River
⭐ State Capital
• City
▢ Colorado
— State Border

United States

Colorado

Hawai'i   Alaska

The Land

The Rocky Mountains reach from Canada almost to Mexico. The Southern Rockies are generally higher than the Middle or Northern Rockies. Formed millions of years ago by **glaciers** and movements in Earth's crust, the Southern Rockies dominate most of western Colorado.

In contrast, eastern Colorado, which is part of the **Great Plains**, is very flat. Because of the lack of rain in the eastern region, this grassy area has very few trees. The plains contain rocky land and **fertile** soil that is washed down from the mountains.

COLORADO RIVER

Red silt colors the water of the Colorado River. *Colorado* means "colored red" in Spanish.

BLACK CANYON

Black Canyon in Gunnison National Park reaches a depth of 2,722 feet.

THE MAROON BELLS

The Maroon Bells are two peaks near Aspen. They are made of mudstone, which gives them a unique color but makes them dangerous to climb. The rock breaks easily.

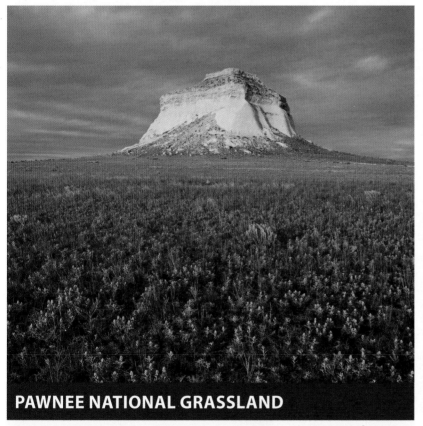

PAWNEE NATIONAL GRASSLAND

Pawnee National Grassland, in northeastern Colorado, is one of two national grasslands in the state.

More than 50 mountain peaks in Colorado are more than 14,000 feet high. Climbers call these peaks the "fourteeners."

Because of a drought in the 1930s, Colorado farms were a part of the Dust Bowl, which spread across the Great Plains. Fields dried up, and wind blew the topsoil away.

A warm wind called a chinook can quickly raise the temperature in Colorado by 30° to 40° Fahrenheit, melting the snow in winter.

Climate

Because of the Colorado landscape, there can be wide temperature variations between places within a short distance of each other. For example, Las Animas is about 90 miles southeast of Pikes Peak, yet there is a difference of 35 degrees Fahrenheit in annual mean temperature. Generally, the higher a mountain, the colder it is at the top. The plains are warm in the summer but dry, cold, and windy in winter.

There is a lot of **precipitation** in the mountains, which is essential for the growth of trees and other plants. Mountain rain and snow also feed the rivers that flow through the state. Snow is present on some peaks year-round. Yet the plains are semiarid.

Average Annual Precipitation Across Colorado

In Boulder, Colorado Springs, Durango, and Pueblo, precipitation varies from about 12 to 20 inches. Some areas of the state have been known to receive as little as 7 inches or as much as 46 inches. Why, do you think, is there so much variation?

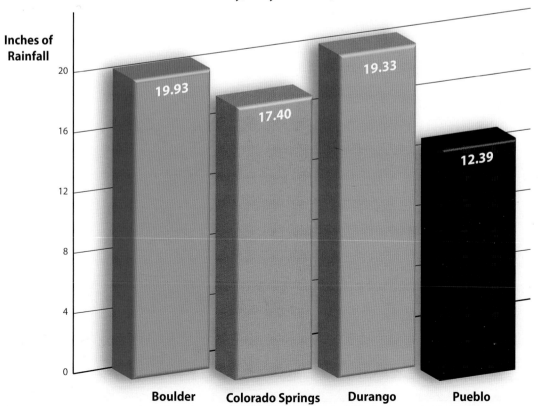

Inches of Rainfall

Boulder	Colorado Springs	Durango	Pueblo
19.93	17.40	19.33	12.39

Natural Resources

L ying within Colorado's mountains and running down their jagged surfaces are two of the state's most important natural resources. They are minerals and rivers. The mining of minerals is a big business in Colorado. Rivers, formed by melting snow and rainfall, flow toward land at lower elevations. The rivers **irrigate** farms and are used as drinking water.

In the dry southwestern states, rivers are a precious resource, so the use of water from Colorado's rivers is **regulated**. The Colorado River flows 1,450 miles across the western United States and into Mexico. Although this river begins in Colorado, the state is allowed to use only a certain amount of water and must leave the rest to flow out of the state. The Colorado River alone supplies water to seven other states and to Mexico.

Water from Colorado's rivers is used in other states for crops and for drinking.

Minerals are natural resources mainly found in Colorado's mountains. The discovery of silver and gold in the Rockies brought some of the first settlers to the area. Later, coal mines provided a reason to stay. More recent discoveries have continued in the state. Molybdenum, a mineral that makes steel stronger, is now a valuable resource for Colorado.

The state of Colorado is trying to get federal approval for a plan to divert additional water from its river systems. The water would be used to enlarge one of the current reservoirs and to fill a new one.

Near the end of World War II, atomic weapons were being developed. At that time, Colorado became an important supplier of two rare metallic elements, uranium and plutonium.

Citizens have tried to persuade the Colorado government to pass a law banning the use of the chemical cyanide in gold mining. Cyanide is used in open-pit mining. People are afraid that the dangerous chemical will leak into the water supply.

Of the 10 active coal mines in western Colorado, three are surface mines and seven are underground mines.

In 1894 one of the largest silver nuggets found in the United States was discovered in Aspen.

Water rights in Colorado are handled by a special system of Water Courts.

Plants

Grasses that can survive without much water cover Colorado's dry eastern plains. Buffalo grass bursts out of the ground after spring rainfalls. Plants that grow in dry conditions, including the yucca plant and the prickly pear, are also found on the grasslands. Cottonwood grows along the edges of streams where the soil is moist.

Farther up in the mountains, quaking aspen, Douglas fir, and blue spruce forests cover the land. The Ponderosa pine, which is the state's most valuable timber tree, grows on the lower mountain slopes. Very few plants take root above the tree line, the elevation above which trees no longer grow. Plants that do grow above the tree line hug the ground to stay out of the cold wind.

COTTONWOOD

The cottonwood is one of the few trees that can withstand Colorado's dry and windy conditions.

ALPINE SUNFLOWERS

Alpine sunflowers spend years storing energy so they can blossom for a few days.

WHITE AND LAVENDER COLUMBINE

The state flower's yellow center is considered a symbol for the gold mining that was done in the state.

BUFFALO GRASS

As the sun dries the earth after rain, buffalo grass becomes **dormant** to await the next rain shower

Cacti grow in the driest areas of Colorado. About 25 species of spine-covered cacti can be found growing naturally.

The law allows only limited grazing by cattle on national grasslands, a specific number of trees to be cut down in national forests, and limited access for vehicles in national parks. The purpose is to save Colorado's environment from overuse.

One-third of all land in the state is government-owned. Picking wildflowers on public land is against the law in Colorado.

Animals

Most animals that live in the Rockies do not stay in just one area. They move up to higher elevations in the summer and are forced down into the valleys in the winter in search of shelter and food.

Herds of elks, deer, and pronghorn antelope roam the plains. Jackrabbits hop, prairie dogs scurry, and rattlesnakes slither among the grasses. Among the trees in the mountains, coyotes find shelter and elks munch on **vegetation**. The steep mountain peaks are the stomping grounds of bighorn sheep, which share the area with tiny mammals called pikas.

PRAIRIE DOGS

Prairie dogs got their name because of the doglike yipping sound they make when they feel they are in danger.

BIG HORN SHEEP

Rocky Mountain big horn sheep, the state animal, use their curled horns to crash against others in battle. They never shed their horns.

PEREGRINE FALCON

The peregrine falcon, the world's fastest bird, soars through Colorado's skies. It can reach speeds of 200 miles per hour while diving.

GRIZZLY BEAR

The grizzly bear is a Colorado mammal classified as **endangered** by the U.S. government. Other Colorado mammals on the list include the wolverine, lynx, and black-footed ferret.

The canyons of northwestern Colorado have the largest collection of **fossilized** dinosaur bones from the **Jurassic period**. *Stegosaurus* was a plant-eating dinosaur that roamed Colorado during that time. It is now the state fossil.

Dinosaur National Monument, on the Utah-Colorado border, has one of the world's largest deposits of dinosaur fossils.

Tourism

When many people think of Colorado, they think of the white, fluffy "powder" on the slopes. This special snow has made Colorado's high peaks and the resorts of Aspen and Vail world-famous. Colorado's challenging ski slopes draw millions of tourists into the state from October to May, for ski season. Winter carnivals include ski races and ski jumping.

Residents spend the summer months in Colorado camping, mountain climbing, white-water rafting, and fishing. These outdoor pursuits also draw a large number of visitors from across the nation. Millions of tourists visit the Colorado wilderness each year.

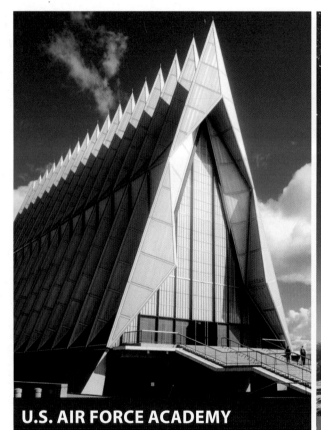

U.S. AIR FORCE ACADEMY

The U.S. Air Force Academy, in Colorado Springs, is perhaps the top human-made attraction in the state. The unique design of its chapel includes 17 aluminum spires that are 150 feet high.

SKI RESORTS

Most Colorado ski resorts are ready with snow in November. Some open as early as late September or early October, though the exact timing varies each year.

FOUR CORNERS MONUMENT

Four Corners Monument in southwestern Colorado allows visitors to stand in four states at one time. Utah, Arizona, New Mexico, and Colorado all meet at one point.

CAVE OF THE WINDS

In the Cave of the Winds, visitors can wander through underground rooms and roam through tunnels lined with **stalagmites** and **stalactites**.

I DIDN'T KNOW THAT!

With two dozen major ski areas, Colorado is the nation's leading ski-resort region.

Pikes Peak was a landmark for settlers heading westward. Today, visitors can drive a car, ride a bicycle, or take a **cog** railway to the top of this famous mountain.

The Royal Gorge Bridge, built in 1929, was the highest suspension bridge in the world at the time it was completed. It is almost a quarter of a mile long and stands almost 1,000 feet above the Royal Gorge canyon.

Industry

Farming and ranching occupied the state's settlers, and much of Colorado industry is still tied to crops and animals. Farming began almost as soon as the first American pioneers arrived in the 1800s. East of the Rocky Mountains, the grasslands are still divided into thousands of farms. On Colorado ranches, beef cattle graze on grass as they have for more than 100 years. Dairy cattle are used for their milk. Plenty of Colorado beef is now fattened in feedlots, however.

Industries in Colorado
Value of Goods and Services in Millions of Dollars

Colorado has many industries tied to the natural resources of the state. However, professional and technical services are fast becoming a greater part of the industry pie, as are "soft" industries such as real estate, finance, and insurance. What is one reason this might be so?

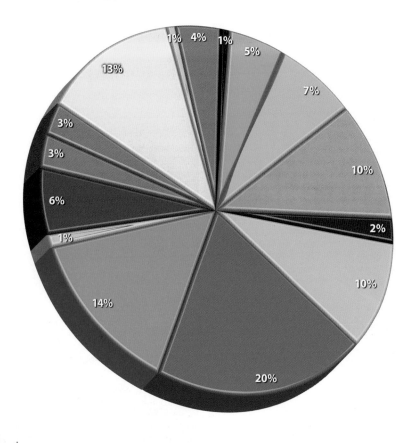

LEGEND

Agriculture, Forestry, and Fishing	$2,069
Mining	$9,813
Utilities	$3,435
Construction	$11,527
Manufacturing	$17,624
Wholesale and Retail Trade	$26,577
Transportation	$6,343
Media and Entertainment	$24,854
Finance, Insurance, and Real Estate	$50,447
Professional and Technical Services	$36,391
Education	$1,781
Health Care	$15,140
Hotels and Restaurants	$8,008
Other Services	$6,560
Government	$32,086
TOTAL	**$252,655**

Large numbers of sheep are being raised in the state for their meat and wool. The sciences that relate to farming and ranching also are part of the state's wide-ranging industries.

The mining, logging, and the manufacturing of wood, metal, and mineral products employ many other Coloradans, as it has for centuries. However, manufacturing has grown to include technological products, such as computers and aerospace equipment. What's more, the service industries now drive the economy. The state is now known for information technology, financial services, medical services, and related fields. The Colorado economy is based on diverse businesses.

Colorado ranks fourth in the nation for sunflower production. The seeds are used for birdseed, snack foods, and in cooking oil production.

Corn, wheat, and hay are the primary crops. Corn and wheat are grown using either irrigation or special farming techniques that make the most of the area's limited moisture.

New industries in Colorado include photonics, which is the application of the energy of light.

The meatpacking industry employs thousands of people in Greeley. Nearby feedlots may contain more than 100,000 steers at a time. Steers are sometimes fattened to a weight of more than 1,000 pounds.

Missiles designed for use in space are developed in Colorado.

Goods and Services

The goods produced in Colorado often fall into one of three categories. The state produces a great deal of scientific equipment, such as heart monitors and military weapons. A second category of goods includes more widely used machinery and technology, such as computers. A third type of product includes food and beverages. For instance, soda pop and packed meat are important moneymakers for the state.

Colorado is a prime location for technological companies. Many computer software developers, programmers, and manufacturers have made Colorado their home. However, the service sector, including tourism, employs more people than any other part of the economy. Large companies attract visitors to the state, as do the state's many recreational facilities. Conventions help keep people in the tourism and service industries busy.

The North American Aerospace Defense Command monitors the sky for air attacks. Its headquarters are located at Peterson Air Force Base, in Colorado Springs.

Apples are one of the most common fruits grown in the state, along with cantaloupes. Potatoes, onions, and beans are the main vegetable crops.

Bankers, lawyers, waiters, and ski-lift operators are all members of the state's service sector. Many Coloradans work for the government, which is also included as part of services in the state's economy. Military personnel, along with the health care workers who care for them and the schoolteachers who teach their children, are all part of the state's enormous service sector.

The military's presence is strong. The Air Force Academy, several Air Force and Army bases, and the North American Aerospace Defense Command, or NORAD, are based in the state.

I DIDN'T KNOW THAT!

NORAD's command center was completed in 1966. The center is well protected, lying more than 1,000 feet beneath Cheyenne Mountain.

The Coors Brewery in Golden is considered the largest single-site facility of its kind in the world.

Gambling, which is legal in certain towns, brings millions of dollars into the state each year.

Famous Coloradans include Ruth Handler, who created the world-famous Barbie® doll in 1959, and David Packard, cofounder of Hewlett-Packard, a large computer-manufacturing company. He was born in Pueblo in 1912.

The military and related businesses directly and indirectly impact about a third of the economy in and around Colorado Springs.

American Indians

American Indians known as the Basket Makers lived in caves in the cliffs of southwestern Colorado as far back as 3,500 years ago. They were skilled at making watertight baskets from materials at hand, such as grass and twigs. Another name for this group is the Ancestral Puebloan people. They have also been called the Anasazi, which is a Navajo word meaning "ancient ones" or "ancient enemies."

In about the year 700, the Ancestral Puebloans moved into structures known as adobes. These shared homes, made of mud and straw, were two or three stories high. The adobes had many connected rooms, which formed unique villages. Some of these pueblos, as early Spanish visitors called the villages, had more than 200 rooms. The Ancestral Puebloans became known as the Cliff Dwellers.

The Ute did not originally wear feather warbonnets, but over time they adopted the style from Plains Indians such as the Sioux.

Later Indian groups in what is now Colorado were often known as Plains Indians or Great Basin Indians, based on where they lived. The Plains Indians of eastern Colorado were mainly the Arapaho and Cheyenne. The Great Basin Indians were mainly the Ute. The Ute lived in Colorado's mountains and valleys. They hunted and gathered food from the land.

In the 1500s, Spanish explorers from Mexico arrived on horseback, and the horse became important to the American Indians of Colorado. By the late 1800s, many of the American Indians had been chased from the land by white American settlers. However, their influence is still felt and reflected in Coloradan culture.

Cliff Palace is the name for one of the largest Ancestral Puebloan cliff dwellings. It had 150 rooms and can be seen at Mesa Verde National Park.

I DIDN'T KNOW THAT!

The first contact American Indians had with the Spanish in Colorado was deadly. Many Indians died of diseases, such as smallpox, brought by the Spanish.

Around the year 1300, several factors may have forced the Ancestral Puebloans to move from Colorado. These factors included drought, lack of resources, and a changing climate.

The Arapaho, Cheyenne, and Ute aided early European explorers. Their knowledge of where to find fresh water and food helped the explorers survive.

Ben Nighthorse Campbell of Colorado, who served in the U.S. Senate from 1993 to 2005, was the only U.S. senator of American Indian ancestry during that time.

Several days after first spotting Pikes Peak in 1806, Zebulon Pike tried to climb the mountain with a band of men. The group had to turn around because of heavy snow.

Explorers

In search of gold, the Spanish explored Colorado in the mid-1500s. They claimed eastern Colorado as their own but moved on. A French explorer claimed the same area in 1682, but again, no permanent settlements were made.

In 1803, in the Louisiana Purchase, the United States bought from France a huge area of land that included eastern Colorado. Eager to see the new American property, U.S. explorers came from the East, including Army officer Zebulon Pike. In 1806, after weeks of crossing flat plains, he was awestruck when he came upon a tremendous mountain, which was later named Pikes Peak after him.

Explorers such as Pike traveled to Colorado and wrote about it so that people from the eastern United States could learn through their experiences. Their early reports claimed that the area was too dry for farming, however, so few settlers followed until gold was found.

Timeline of Settlement

Interest Increases

1803 After the Louisiana Purchase, exploration of what is now Colorado begins in earnest.

Early Exploration

1805 U.S. soldier Zebulon Pike is sent by the government to map the area and record scientific information.

1820 Major Stephen Long leads an expedition that explores the Colorado plains. With him is Samuel Seymour, perhaps the first American to paint pictures of the Colorado Rockies. Fur traders and trappers are the first to follow the explorers' lead.

1842 U.S. Army lieutenant John C. Frémont, with the help of famous frontier scout Kit Carson, explores the Rocky Mountain region, including part of Colorado.

First Settlements

1858 Gold is discovered along the South Platte River. Gold-mining towns pop up, including Central City, Black Hawk, Gold Hill, and Cripple Creek.

Conflict and Change

1861 The U.S. Congress establishes the Colorado Territory, with the same boundaries as the present-day state. Soon after, the Civil War breaks out. Over the course of the war, about 4,000 Coloradans volunteer for the Union Army.

1864 In the Sand Creek Massacre, Colorado volunteer soldiers kill more than 150 American Indian men, women, and children. The event is part of a growing conflict between settlers and American Indians as the number of settlers increases.

1876 President Ulysses S. Grant signs papers making Colorado the 38th state.

Early Settlers

I n the early 1800s, Colorado "mountain men" trapped beaver and other fur-bearing animals. They also traded with American Indians for beaver pelts, used to make hats, and for buffalo hides, which were made into robes and other items.

Map of Settlements and Resources in Early Colorado

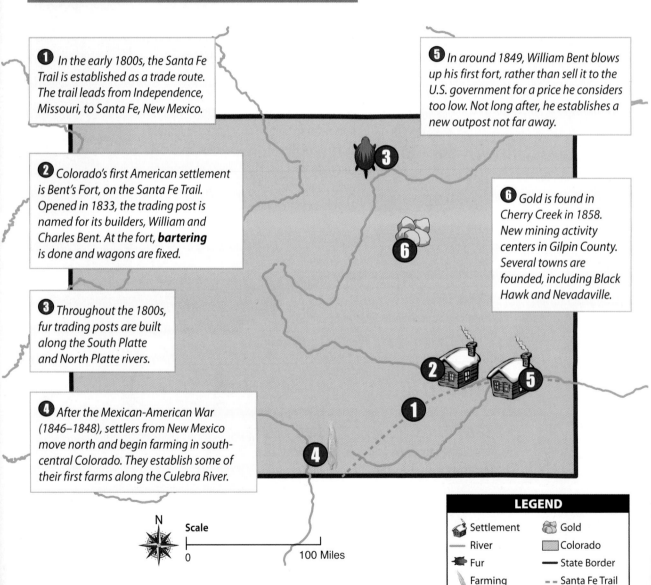

① In the early 1800s, the Santa Fe Trail is established as a trade route. The trail leads from Independence, Missouri, to Santa Fe, New Mexico.

② Colorado's first American settlement is Bent's Fort, on the Santa Fe Trail. Opened in 1833, the trading post is named for its builders, William and Charles Bent. At the fort, **bartering** is done and wagons are fixed.

③ Throughout the 1800s, fur trading posts are built along the South Platte and North Platte rivers.

④ After the Mexican-American War (1846–1848), settlers from New Mexico move north and begin farming in south-central Colorado. They establish some of their first farms along the Culebra River.

⑤ In around 1849, William Bent blows up his first fort, rather than sell it to the U.S. government for a price he considers too low. Not long after, he establishes a new outpost not far away.

⑥ Gold is found in Cherry Creek in 1858. New mining activity centers in Gilpin County. Several towns are founded, including Black Hawk and Nevadaville.

N

Scale
0   100 Miles

LEGEND

🪨 Settlement		🪙 Gold	
— River		▢ Colorado	
🦫 Fur		— State Border	
🌿 Farming		- - Santa Fe Trail	

Mexico gained control of western Colorado in 1821 when Mexico won its independence from Spain. The United States and Mexico fought the Mexican-American War from 1846 to 1848. When the United States won the war, a huge area of the Southwest, including western Colorado, became part of the United States.

After gold was found in Cherry Creek, a town sprang up. Today it is known as Denver. Mining camps began popping up in the Rockies. Storekeepers set up shops, providing goods to prospectors and getting gold in return.

Settlers heading westward at that time were often blocked by the mountains, so they set up houses in the eastern foothills, where the majority of Coloradans live today. The settlers fought with American Indians for control of the land. The newcomers convinced the U.S. government to make Colorado a territory in 1861, and the U.S. Army stepped in to fight the original inhabitants. By the 1880s, most American Indians had been forced onto **reservations** or driven away.

Prospectors came to Colorado in search of precious metals and personal fortune.

I DIDN'T KNOW THAT!

The site of the 1864 Sand Creek Massacre is now a National Historic Site preserved by the National Park Service.

In 1873, William Henry Jackson photographed the Mount of the Holy Cross, a 14,005-foot mountain with two snowy **crevices** shaped like a huge cross. Thousands of people have since climbed a nearby mountain to see it.

The influence of Spanish and Mexican explorers and settlers is apparent in the Spanish names of some Colorado places, such as the city of Pueblo and the Sangre de Cristo Mountains.

San Luis was founded in 1851 by Hispanic settlers hoping to ranch and farm.

After explorer Zebulon Pike entered the Spanish territory of New Mexico in July 1806, he was captured and imprisoned. He was released in July 1807.

William Bent's trading company bought and sold Mexican blankets, buffalo robes, sheep, and horses. Furs sold by mountain men wound up as far away as Europe.

Notable People

The state of Colorado has been the birthplace or adopted home of numerous notable Americans. Though Colorado is relatively new, compared with states in the East, and has had fewer generations of leaders, Coloradans have made important contributions in the arts, politics, science, sports, the military, and more. Many Coloradans who helped develop their state historically also participated in meaningful ways to the development of the nation and the national character.

BYRON R. WHITE (1917–2002)

Supreme Court Justice Byron R. White, appointed by President John F. Kennedy, served on the High Court from 1962 to 1993. He remains the only justice to also be given a Heisman Trophy, awarded to the best collegiate football player. "Whizzer" White won for his performance as a halfback at the University of Colorado. He played professionally in the same position for the Pittsburg Pirates, now the Pittsburgh Steelers.

WILLIAM JACKSON PALMER (1838–1909)

William Palmer served in the Union Army during the Civil War and helped the freed slaves afterward. He then moved to the West, cofounding the Denver and Rio Grande Railroad. Palmer founded the town of Colorado Springs. He also helped establish the Colorado School for the Deaf and Blind and the University of Colorado at Colorado Springs.

PATRICIA SCHROEDER (1940–)

Representing a Denver-area district, Patricia Schroeder served twelve terms in the U.S. House of Representatives, from 1973 to 1997. She was one of the first women to be appointed to the House Armed Services Committee, where she was vocal about women's rights in the military and military spending. She was cochair of the Congressional Caucus for Women's Issues.

FLORENCE RENA SABIN (1871–1953)

Florence Rena Sabin was a pioneer in medicine. The first female graduate and full professor at Johns Hopkins University School of Medicine, Sabin was an important medical researcher. Her work with blood cells and the immune system broke new ground, making her the first female elected to the National Academy of Sciences.

NATHANIEL P. HILL (1832–1900)

As a professor of chemistry at Brown University, in Rhode Island, Nathaniel P. Hill traveled to Colorado to study minerals and became successful in the businesses of smelting and real estate. Hill was a U.S. senator from 1879 to 1885 and on the U.S. delegation to the International Monetary Commission in 1891.

Condoleezza Rice (1954–), the first African American woman to serve as national security adviser and secretary of state, moved to Denver with her family in 1967. She attended the University of Denver, where her father was an assistant dean.

John L. Swigert (1931–1982), who was born in Denver, became an astronaut. He was on the crew of *Apollo 13*, which returned safely to Earth after an oxygen tank ruptured. Swigert served as the executive director of the Committee on Science and Technology of the U.S. House of Representatives. After leaving NASA, he was elected to the U.S. Congress but died before taking office.

Population

When Colorado became a territory, there were 34,000 people in the area. The population leaped from 40,000 in 1870 to almost 200,000 in 1880. Over the years, similar growth spurts have occurred. As industries such as tourism and military defense have grown, new people have flooded into the state. In 2000, Colorado's population was about 4.3 million. By 2010, the number of Coloradans had grown to 5,029,196.

Despite the beauty of Colorado's wild areas, most Coloradans live in cities. The high population density has led to environmental challenges, including air pollution and water shortages.

Colorado Population 1950–2010

Colorado's population is almost four times as large as it was in 1950. What are some of the reasons the state has seen such rapid growth?

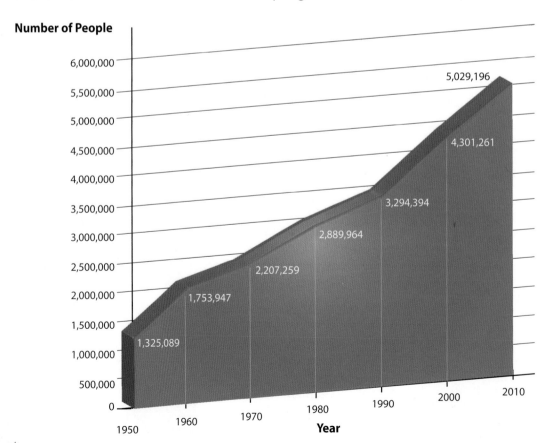

Number of People

6,000,000
5,500,000 — 5,029,196
5,000,000
4,500,000 — 4,301,261
4,000,000
3,500,000 — 3,294,394
3,000,000 — 2,889,964
2,500,000 — 2,207,259
2,000,000 — 1,753,947
1,500,000
1,000,000 — 1,325,089
500,000
0

1950 1960 1970 1980 1990 2000 2010

Year

With many vehicles and factories releasing pollutants, a brown smog often hovers over Denver. Colorado's mountains trap the smog, preventing it from blowing away.

The majority of Coloradans live in the Front Range, which is on the eastern edge of the Rocky Mountains. The Front Range contains the largest cities in the state.

The capital city of Denver is one of the twenty-five largest cities in the United States, with a population of more than 600,000 people.

High population density has caused water shortages. Coloradans are working on finding ways to provide enough water and keep the state's rivers healthy.

Silverton Mountain is in San Juan, the least populated county. San Juan sits on both sides of the Continental Divide.

Politics and Government

Colorado's state government has three branches. They are the executive, legislative, and judicial branches. The executive branch is led by the governor, who is responsible for enforcing the state's laws and has the power to turn down, or veto, new laws passed by the legislature. The governor and other top officials in the executive branch are elected for four-year terms.

Denver is a consolidated city-county. This means it is a city and county in one legal authority. Usually, a city is a municipal corporation separate from the state. A county is an administrative division of the state. The state of Colorado recognizes Denver as both.

The legislature, which is called the General Assembly, is made up of a 35-member Senate and a 65-member House of Representatives. A law turned down by the governor can still be passed if two-thirds of both senators and representatives approve it.

The judicial branch consists of the courts. Colorado's highest court is the Supreme Court. Supreme Court judges are elected to 10-year terms. The judiciary also includes the Colorado Court of Appeals and district and county courts.

The Colorado State Capitol, located in Denver, was built to look like the United States Capitol. The Colorado Capitol was opened in 1894.

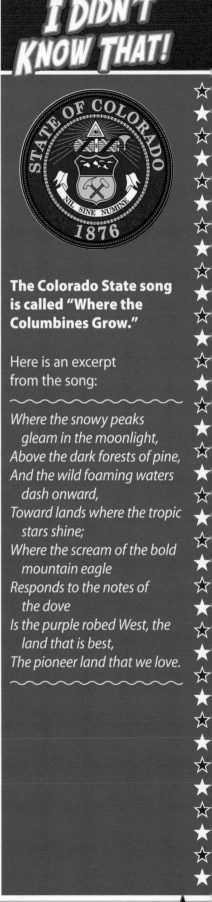

I DIDN'T KNOW THAT!

The Colorado State song is called "Where the Columbines Grow."

Here is an excerpt from the song:

*Where the snowy peaks
   gleam in the moonlight,
Above the dark forests of pine,
And the wild foaming waters
   dash onward,
Toward lands where the tropic
   stars shine;
Where the scream of the bold
   mountain eagle
Responds to the notes of
   the dove
Is the purple robed West, the
   land that is best,
The pioneer land that we love.*

Cultural Groups

Hispanics, or people from a Spanish-speaking culture, make up about 20 percent of Colorado's population. The national average is about 16 percent. Mexicans were among the first permanent settlers in Colorado. They traveled from New Mexico in search of places to farm and ranch. On Colorado's vast plains, land and work were plentiful. Hispanics have lived in the state ever since. Some speak both Spanish and English, and they continue to keep their culture and traditions strong, including special holidays.

One such holiday is Cinco de Mayo. In a huge battle in 1862 on Mexican territory, the Mexican army was outnumbered three to one. A French army had come to take over the land. Although their army was larger, the French were defeated. This occurred on Cinco de Mayo, or May 5. Today the victory is celebrated throughout Colorado's Hispanic community, with Mexican food, drinks, and dancing.

Denver boasts one of the largest Cinco de Mayo celebrations in the United States. The event draws about 400,000 attendees.

Hispanic culture stands out in the state, but there are other cultures in the mix, including Asian cultures. Many Japanese immigrants moved to the United States to help build the railroads. After the railroad work ended, some stayed for farm work. By the 1900s, most Japanese Americans in Colorado were living and working on farms. The terrible droughts and heat waves of the 1930s were a difficult time for all farmers, and later, during World War II, Japanese Americans faced even greater hardships. The U.S. government placed Japanese Americans in **internment camps** until the war ended. Asian Americans now make up about 3 percent of Colorado's population.

American Indians now make up only about 1 percent of the state's population, but their influence can still be felt. When European explorers reached Colorado's mountains and grasslands, they found these areas already inhabited. The Ute, Arapaho, and Cheyenne had lived there for many generations. Indian reservations in Colorado today are the Ute Mountain Ute Reservation and the Southern Ute Reservation.

Powwows, or intertribal American Indian celebrations, are held in Colorado throughout the year.

Arts and Entertainment

Set among red rock formations that were formed about 70 million years ago, the Red Rocks Amphitheatre is a 9,000-seat outdoor theater west of Denver that hosts jazz, rock, folk, and classical concerts. The concert space provides a beautiful backdrop of Colorado scenery.

To explore Colorado scenery, visitors can take a historic train ride. Some train tours follow the same track that gold miners used in the 1800s. For even more action, people can hop aboard a dogsled and be carried through the forest by a team of huskies. Many sled dogs are kenneled and trained in the state.

The first organized concerts at the Red Rocks Amphitheatre took place in the early 1900s.

Colorado's entertainment scene includes cowboys at the National Western Stock Show and Rodeo, a rodeo and horse show held annually in Denver. Six Flags Elitch Gardens, an amusement park in Denver, features roller coasters and other rides. William Shakespeare's plays are brought to life in a summer festival at the University of Colorado at Boulder. The Central City Opera tells stories in song, just as it has almost every year since 1878.

Museums offer a variety of sights and experiences. The Children's Museum of Denver gives kids hands-on opportunities to try new things, such as learning how to fill a car with gasoline. People can examine 10,000-year-old spearheads used to hunt bison or 150-million-year-old dinosaur bones in the Colorado History Museum. The Denver Art Museum houses one of the finest collections of American Indian art in the world. The Fine Arts Center of Colorado Springs offers art celebrating the contributions of many ethnic groups.

Grammy winner India.Arie was born in Denver as India Arie Simpson. She has gained fame as a singer, songwriter, instrumentalist, and music producer.

Sports

Winter sports, particularly skiing and snowboarding, draw millions of visitors to Colorado annually. In warmer weather, kayakers and rafters tackle the white water of the state's wild rivers, dodging jagged rocks when successful or flipping over when not. At Great Sand Dunes National Monument, snowboarders and skiers go down hills of hot sand. Rock climbers scale cliffs near Boulder, with the weight of their bodies hanging from fingertips and toes as they move up the rock face. At the Ouray Ice Park, ice climbers scale frozen waterfalls with ropes and pickaxes. Colorado's extreme sports, recreational activities, and spectator sports bring tourists back year after year.

White-water rafting is a popular way to see the stunning scenery of the state.

More moderate sports enthusiasts enjoy fly fishing in slow-moving streams. Others hike the Garden of the Gods for a breathtaking experience. The red sandstone rocks in the "garden" have been sculpted by wind and rain into unusual shapes.

For those who enjoy watching sports, Denver is the place to be. The Colorado Avalanche hocky team represents Colorado in the National Hockey League and won the Stanley Cup in 1996 and 2001. The Colorado Rockies are Denver's Major League Baseball team. The Denver Nuggets play in the National Basketball Association. The Colorado Rapids was one of the original teams when Major League Soccer was founded in 1995. The Denver Broncos of the National Football League have appeared in six Super Bowls. These teams are the pride and joy of Coloradans, along with the state's collegiate and other amateur teams, which include the U.S. Olympians at the U.S. Olympic Training Complex in Colorado Springs.

At Ouray, ice climbers can work out on the face of the rock, then relax in a hot spring.

National Averages Comparison

The United States is a federal republic, consisting of fifty states and the District of Columbia. Alaska and Hawai'i are the only non-contiguous, or non-touching, states in the nation. Today, the United States of America is the third-largest country in the world in population. The United States Census Bureau takes a census, or count of all the people, every ten years. It also regularly collects other kinds of data about the population and the economy. How does Colorado compare to the national average?

Comparison Chart

United States 2010 Census Data *	USA	Colorado
Admission to Union	NA	August 1, 1876
Land Area (in square miles)	3,537,438.44	103,717.53
Population Total	308,745,538	5,029,196
Population Density (people per square mile)	87.28	48.49
Population Percentage Change (April 1, 2000, to April 1, 2010)	9.7%	16.9%
White Persons (percent)	72.4%	81.3%
Black Persons (percent)	12.6%	4.0%
American Indian and Alaska Native Persons (percent)	0.9%	1.1%
Asian Persons (percent)	4.8%	2.8%
Native Hawaiian and Other Pacific Islander Persons (percent)	0.2%	0.1%
Some Other Race (percent)	6.2%	7.2%
Persons Reporting Two or More Races (percent)	2.9%	3.4%
Persons of Hispanic or Latino Origin (percent)	16.3%	20.7%
Not of Hispanic or Latino Origin (percent)	83.7%	79.3%
Median Household Income	$52,029	$57,184
Percentage of People Age 25 or Over Who Have Graduated from High School	80.4%	86.9%

*All figures are based on the 2010 United States Census, with the exception of the last two items. Percentages may not add to 100 because of rounding.

How to Improve My Community

Strong communities make strong states. Think about what features are important in your community. What do you value? Education? Health? Forests? Safety? Beautiful spaces? Government works to help citizens create ideal living conditions that are fair to all by providing services in communities. Consider what changes you could make in your community. How would they improve your state as a whole? Using this concept web as a guide, write a report that outlines the features you think are most important in your community and what improvements could be made. A strong state needs strong communities.

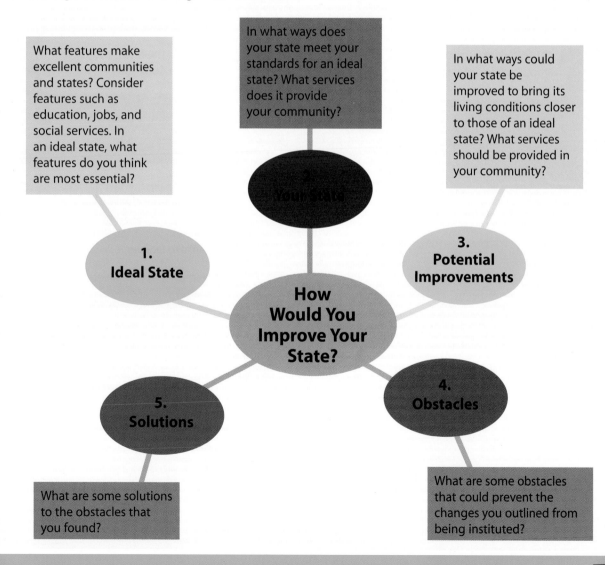

What features make excellent communities and states? Consider features such as education, jobs, and social services. In an ideal state, what features do you think are most essential?

In what ways does your state meet your standards for an ideal state? What services does it provide your community?

In what ways could your state be improved to bring its living conditions closer to those of an ideal state? What services should be provided in your community?

2. Your State

1. Ideal State

3. Potential Improvements

How Would You Improve Your State?

5. Solutions

4. Obstacles

What are some solutions to the obstacles that you found?

What are some obstacles that could prevent the changes you outlined from being instituted?

Exercise Your Mind!

Think about these questions and then use your research skills to find the answers and learn more fascinating facts about Colorado. A teacher, librarian, or parent may be able to help you locate the best sources to use in your research.

5 Who popularized the phrase "Go West, young man"?

1 What is the Continental Divide?

2 When did oil become important in Colorado?

6 When did the first newspaper appear in Colorado?

3 How long is the Colorado River?

7 True or False? Singer Henry John Deutschendorf loved Colorado so much, he wrote songs about the state and changed his last name to Denver.

4 What draws tourists to the Sangre de Cristo Mountains?

8 Which woman, who made a fortune in Colorado silver, became known as "unsinkable"?

Words to Know

bartering: trading without money

capitol: building for the legislature

cog: a notch on the rim of a wheel

crevices: narrow and deep cracks

density: the quantity of anything per unit of area

dormant: in a state of inactivity

elevation: height above Earth's surface

endangered: at risk of becoming extinct, or completely dying out

fertile: capable of producing plants and crops

fossilized: preserved from a past geologic age

geothermal: heated from inside Earth

glacier: a large mass of ice formed when snowfall is greater than summer melting

Great Plains: vast flat lands that extend from the Mississippi River to the Rocky Mountains and from Canada to Mexico

internment camps: temporary camps to imprison people, for example, those that held Japanese Americans during World War II

irrigate: to supply land with water

Jurassic period: a period of time that lasted from 208 million to 144 million years ago

precipitation: water that falls as rain or snow

regulated: controlled or directed according to a rule

reservations: areas of protected land, such as those set aside for American Indians

stalactites: deposits of minerals that point downward from the roof of a cave or cavern

stalagmites: deposits of minerals that point upward from the floor of a cave or cavern

vegetation: plant life

Index

alpine sunflowers 16

Ancestral Puebloans 26, 27

Arapaho 27, 39

Bent, William 30, 31

Bent's Fort 30

Brown, Clara 39

buffalo grass 17

Cheyenne 27, 39

Cinco de Mayo 38

Colorado River 8, 10, 15, 46

Denver 5, 8, 9, 20, 31, 33, 35, 36, 38, 40, 41, 43, 46

dinosaur 19, 40

gold 4, 28, 29, 30, 31, 36, 39, 40

Great Plains 10

Long, Stephen 29

molybdenum 15

Mount Elbert 7

NORAD 24, 25

peregrine falcon 19

Pike, Zebulon 21, 28

Pikes Peak 13, 21, 28, 39

plutonium 15

population 9, 34, 35, 38, 39, 44

Red Rocks Amphitheatre 40

Rocky Mountain bighorn sheep 8, 18

Rocky Mountains (Rockies) 4, 6, 7, 10, 11, 14, 15, 18, 22, 31, 35

Royal Gorge Bridge 21

Sand Creek Massacre 29, 31

Stegosaurus 19

Ute 27, 39

Log on to www.av2books.com

AV² by Weigl brings you media enhanced books that support active learning. Go to www.av2books.com, and enter the special code found on page 2 of this book. You will gain access to enriched and enhanced content that supplements and complements this book. Content includes video, audio, web links, quizzes, a slide show, and activities.

Audio
Listen to sections of the book read aloud.

Video
Watch informative video clips.

Embedded Weblinks
Gain additional information for research.

Try This!
Complete activities and hands-on experiments.

WHAT'S ONLINE?

Try This!	Embedded Weblinks	Video	EXTRA FEATURES
Test your knowledge of the state in a mapping activity.	Discover more attractions in Colorado.	Watch a video introduction to Colorado.	**Audio** Listen to sections of the book read aloud.
Find out more about precipitation in your city.	Learn more about the history of the state.	Watch a video about the features of the state.	**Key Words** Study vocabulary, and complete a matching word activity.
Plan what attractions you would like to visit in the state.	Learn the full lyrics of the state song.		
Learn more about the early natural resources of the state.			**Slide Show** View images and captions, and prepare a presentation.
Write a biography about a notable resident of Colorado.			
Complete an educational census activity.			**Quizzes** Test your knowledge.

AV² was built to bridge the gap between print and digital. We encourage you to tell us what you like and what you want to see in the future.

Sign up to be an AV² Ambassador at www.av2books.com/ambassador.

Due to the dynamic nature of the Internet, some of the URLs and activities provided as part of AV² by Weigl may have changed or ceased to exist. AV² by Weigl accepts no responsibility for any such changes. All media enhanced books are regularly monitored to update addresses and sites in a timely manner. Contact AV² by Weigl at 1-866-649-3445 or av2books@weigl.com with any questions, comments, or feedback.